"The Wealth Blueprint: A Comprehensive Guide to Achieving Financial Success"

Welcome to "The Wealth Blueprint," a practical and insightful guide that will empower you to embark on a transformative journey toward financial abundance. In this book, we will explore the strategies, mindsets, and actionable steps necessary to attain and sustain wealth. By implementing the principles outlined within these pages, you can pave your path to prosperity and unlock your true potential. Remember, becoming rich goes beyond monetary gains; it encompasses a holistic approach to living a fulfilling and prosperous life.

I0504698

CHAPTER 1: LAYING THE FOUNDATION

- Understanding the concept of wealth: Defining wealth beyond material possessions and embracing abundance in all areas of life.
- Developing a wealth mindset: Cultivating a positive and abundance-oriented mindset that attracts prosperity.
- Identifying your goals: Establishing clear and measurable financial objectives to provide direction and motivation.

CHAPTER 2:
MASTERING PERSONAL FINANCE

- Budgeting and saving: Creating a strategic plan to manage income, expenses, and savings effectively.
- Debt management: Strategies for reducing and eliminating debt to enhance financial stability and freedom.
- Building an emergency fund: Establishing a safety net to handle unexpected expenses and unforeseen circumstances.

CHAPTER 3: GENERATING MULTIPLE STREAMS OF INCOME

- The power of diversification: Understanding the benefits of diversifying income sources to maximize wealth creation.
- Entrepreneurship and business ventures: Unleashing your entrepreneurial spirit and exploring various business opportunities.
- Investing wisely: Learning about different investment vehicles, such as stocks, real estate, and other assets, to grow your wealth.

CHAPTER 4: LEVERAGING TECHNOLOGY AND THE DIGITAL AGE

- Exploring online opportunities: Utilizing the internet to create income streams, such as e-commerce, affiliate marketing, and freelancing.
- The rise of cryptocurrencies: Understanding the potential of digital currencies and how to navigate the cryptocurrency market.
- Embracing automation and scalability: Harnessing the power of technology to streamline processes and amplify your earning potential.

CHAPTER 5: NURTURING RELATIONSHIPS AND NETWORKING

- The value of connections: Leveraging your network to gain insights, opportunities, and support on your wealth-building journey.
- Collaborations and partnerships: Building strategic alliances that can enhance your business ventures and accelerate growth.
- Giving back: The importance of philanthropy and contributing to causes that align with your values.

CHAPTER 6: ACHIEVING FINANCIAL FREEDOM AND LONG-TERM WEALTH

- Financial planning and retirement: Developing a robust financial plan to secure your future and maintain wealth in the long run.
- Continual learning and personal growth: Embracing a mindset of lifelong learning to adapt to changing economic landscapes and seize new opportunities.
- Balancing wealth and well-being: Finding harmony between financial success, personal well-being, and meaningful relationships.

"The Wealth Blueprint" provides you with the tools, insights, and strategies to embark on a journey toward financial freedom and lasting prosperity. Remember, wealth is not an overnight achievement but a result of consistent effort, determination, and the application of proven principles. As you navigate your path, always remain adaptable, open-minded, and willing to embrace new opportunities. Start now, take action, and unlock the door to the abundant life you deserve.

CHAPTER 1: LAYING THE FOUNDATION

Before embarking on the journey to financial success, it is essential to lay a strong foundation that will support your wealth-building endeavors. In this chapter, we will delve into the fundamental principles and mindset necessary to set yourself up for long-term prosperity.

Section 1: Defining Wealth Beyond Material Possessions

- Shifting your perspective: Understanding that true wealth encompasses more than just accumulating material possessions. It includes physical, mental, and emotional well-being, strong relationships, personal growth, and a sense of purpose.
- Clarifying your values and priorities: Reflecting on what truly matters to you and aligning your financial goals with your values, ensuring that your pursuit of wealth remains meaningful and fulfilling.

Section 2: Cultivating a Wealth Mindset

- Embracing abundance: Adopting a mindset of abundance and recognizing that there are abundant opportunities and resources available to create wealth.
- Overcoming limiting beliefs: Identifying and challenging self-limiting beliefs that may hinder your financial growth. Cultivating a positive and empowering mindset that supports your aspirations.

Section 3: Setting Clear and Measurable Goals

- Defining your vision: Visualizing your desired financial

future and setting specific, measurable, attainable, relevant, and time-bound (SMART) goals that align with your vision.

- Breaking down your goals: Breaking larger goals into smaller, manageable milestones to track progress and maintain motivation.
- Writing a personal mission statement: Crafting a concise statement that encapsulates your financial goals, values, and purpose, serving as a guiding compass throughout your wealth-building journey.

Section 4: Developing Financial Literacy

- Educating yourself: Committing to continuous learning about personal finance, investment strategies, and wealth management to make informed decisions.
- Understanding financial terminology: Familiarizing yourself with key financial concepts, such as compound interest, asset allocation, risk management, and taxation, to navigate the financial landscape effectively.

Section 5: Cultivating Financial Discipline and Responsibility

- Practicing mindful spending: Developing responsible spending habits and distinguishing between wants and needs to prioritize long-term financial goals.
- Saving and investing: Establishing a systematic approach to saving and investing, ensuring that a portion of your income is dedicated to building wealth.
- Building an emergency fund: Creating a safety net to protect against unexpected financial setbacks, such as job loss or medical emergencies.

Section 6: Seeking Professional Guidance

- The role of financial advisors: Understanding when and how to seek professional financial advice to optimize your wealth-building strategy.
- Choosing the right advisor: Evaluating credentials, experience, and alignment with your goals to find a trusted financial advisor who can guide you on your path

to wealth.

Conclusion: By laying a solid foundation, encompassing a holistic understanding of wealth, cultivating a wealth mindset, setting clear goals, and developing financial literacy and discipline, you have established the groundwork for your journey toward financial success. Remember that this chapter is just the beginning—a solid foundation will provide stability and clarity as you progress through the subsequent chapters of "The Wealth Blueprint." Embrace the principles outlined here, stay committed, and get ready to unlock the doors to abundant possibilities that lie ahead.

CHAPTER 2: MASTERING PERSONAL FINANCE

In order to build wealth and achieve financial success, it is crucial to master the principles of personal finance. This chapter will provide you with the knowledge and strategies to effectively manage your money, budget wisely, and make informed financial decisions.

Section 1: Creating a Comprehensive Budget

- Assessing your income and expenses: Analyzing your income sources and tracking your expenses to gain a clear understanding of your financial situation.
- Categorizing expenses: Organizing your expenses into categories (e.g., housing, transportation, groceries, entertainment) to identify areas where you can make adjustments and save money.
- Establishing a budget: Developing a realistic budget that allocates funds to essential expenses, savings, debt repayment, and discretionary spending.

Section 2: Saving and Investing

- Paying yourself first: Prioritizing saving by setting aside a portion of your income before allocating funds to other expenses.
- Building an emergency fund: Creating a separate savings account to cover unexpected expenses, aiming for a reserve of three to six months' worth of living expenses.
- Exploring investment options: Understanding different investment vehicles, such as stocks, bonds, mutual funds,

and real estate, to grow your wealth over time.

Section 3: Debt Management

- Evaluating your debt: Assessing your current debt situation, including outstanding loans, credit card balances, and interest rates.
- Developing a debt repayment strategy: Identifying the most effective approach to paying off debts, such as the avalanche method (prioritizing high-interest debts first) or the snowball method (starting with smaller debts for a psychological boost).
- Minimizing future debt: Adopting responsible borrowing habits, avoiding unnecessary debt, and using credit cards wisely to prevent falling into a debt trap.

Section 4: Optimizing Your Expenses

- Prioritizing needs over wants: Distinguishing between essential and discretionary expenses to make informed spending decisions.
- Negotiating bills and expenses: Seeking opportunities to negotiate lower rates for services, such as utilities, insurance, and subscriptions.
- Practicing mindful spending: Being intentional with your purchases, avoiding impulse buying, and seeking value for money.

Section 5: Tax Planning and Optimization

- Understanding the tax system: Familiarizing yourself with relevant tax laws and regulations to optimize your tax planning strategies.
- Maximizing tax deductions and credits: Taking advantage of available deductions and credits to minimize your tax liability.
- Consulting with tax professionals: Seeking guidance from tax professionals to ensure compliance and identify tax-saving opportunities.

Section 6: Regular Financial Checkups and Adjustments

- Reviewing and reassessing your financial plan: Conducting regular reviews of your budget, savings, and investment strategies to ensure they align with your goals.
- Making necessary adjustments: Modifying your financial plan as circumstances change, such as income fluctuations, life events, or shifting priorities.

Conclusion: Mastering personal finance is a crucial step towards achieving financial success. By creating a comprehensive budget, saving and investing wisely, managing debt effectively, optimizing expenses, and staying proactive with tax planning, you can take control of your financial well-being. Regularly assessing and adjusting your financial strategies will ensure that you stay on track and continue to make progress toward your wealth-building goals. Remember, personal finance is a lifelong journey, and by mastering these principles, you lay the groundwork for long-term financial stability and abundance.

CHAPTER 3:
GENERATING MULTIPLE
STREAMS OF INCOME

In today's dynamic and ever-changing economy, relying on a single source of income may not be sufficient to achieve true financial freedom. This chapter explores the importance of diversifying your income streams and provides strategies for creating multiple avenues of revenue generation.

Section 1: Recognizing the Power of Diversification

- Understanding the benefits of multiple income streams: Exploring the advantages of diversifying your income, including increased financial security, reduced risk, and enhanced wealth-building potential.
- Embracing a mindset of opportunity: Cultivating a mindset that seeks and capitalizes on various income-generating possibilities, both traditional and unconventional.

Section 2: Entrepreneurship and Business Ventures

- Identifying your passions and skills: Assessing your interests, talents, and expertise to uncover potential entrepreneurial opportunities.
- Starting a business: Understanding the fundamentals of starting a business, including market research, business planning, financing options, and marketing strategies.
- Scaling and expanding your business: Exploring methods to grow your business, such as hiring employees, expanding into new markets, or diversifying your product

or service offerings.

Section 3: Investing in Income-Generating Assets

- Real Estate investments: Exploring opportunities in real estate, such as rental properties, real estate investment trusts (REITs), or real estate crowdfunding.
- Stock market investments: Understanding the basics of stock investing, including stocks, bonds, index funds, and dividend-paying companies.
- Peer-to-peer lending and crowdfunding: Exploring alternative investment options, such as peer-to-peer lending platforms or crowdfunding campaigns, to generate passive income.

Section 4: Creating Digital Income Streams

- E-commerce and online businesses: Leveraging the power of the internet to start an online store, sell digital products, or offer online services.
- Affiliate marketing: Partnering with companies to promote their products or services and earning commissions for successful referrals.
- Creating and monetizing digital content: Exploring avenues like blogging, podcasting, vlogging, or writing e-books to generate income through advertising, sponsorships, or product sales.

Section 5: Leveraging Your Skills and Expertise

- Freelancing and consulting: Offering your skills and expertise as a freelancer or consultant in your field of knowledge.
- Teaching and coaching: Sharing your expertise through teaching online courses, offering coaching or mentoring services, or conducting workshops and seminars.
- Monetizing your hobbies and talents: Identifying ways to turn your hobbies or talents into income-generating opportunities, such as photography, art, writing, or music.

Section 6: Balancing Time, Effort, and Return on Investment

- Assessing opportunities: Evaluating potential income streams based on their profitability, scalability, and alignment with your skills and resources.
- Prioritizing and time management: Balancing your time and effort across multiple income streams to ensure effectiveness and avoid burnout.
- Continual learning and adaptation: Staying updated with market trends, technological advancements, and changing consumer demands to remain relevant and maximize your income potential.

Conclusion: Generating multiple streams of income is a powerful strategy to diversify your financial portfolio and accelerate wealth creation. By embracing entrepreneurship, investing in income-generating assets, leveraging the digital landscape, and monetizing your skills and expertise, you can create a robust and resilient income stream ecosystem. Remember, creating multiple income streams requires effort, dedication, and continuous adaptation. It is essential to assess opportunities, manage your time effectively, and stay informed to optimize your returns. With determination and an open mindset, you can unlock the potential for financial abundance and enjoy the freedom and flexibility that come with multiple streams of income.

CHAPTER 4: LEVERAGING TECHNOLOGY AND THE DIGITAL AGE

In the rapidly evolving digital age, technology presents boundless opportunities to create wealth and achieve financial success. This chapter explores the transformative power of technology and provides insights into leveraging digital tools and platforms to maximize your earning potential.

Section 1: The Rise of Online Opportunities

- Understanding the digital landscape: Exploring the vast array of online opportunities and platforms available for income generation.
- E-commerce: Setting up and running an online store to sell products or services globally, leveraging platforms like Shopify, Amazon, or eBay.
- Dropshipping and fulfillment services: Exploring the model of selling products without physically holding inventory, utilizing services like AliExpress or Amazon FBA.

Section 2: Affiliate Marketing and Influencer Partnerships

- Affiliate marketing: Partnering with companies to promote their products or services, earning commissions on successful referrals using platforms like Amazon Associates, ShareASale, or CJ Affiliate.

- Influencer marketing: Building a personal brand and leveraging social media platforms to collaborate with brands and earn income through sponsored content and partnerships.

Section 3: Freelancing and the Gig Economy

- Freelancing platforms: Exploring websites like Upwork, Fiverr, or Freelancer to offer your skills and services to a global client base.
- Gig economy opportunities: Leveraging platforms like Uber, TaskRabbit, or DoorDash to provide on-demand services and generate income.

Section 4: Online Content Creation and Monetization

- Blogging and content creation: Starting a blog or website to share valuable content, attracting an audience and monetizing through advertising, sponsored posts, or selling digital products.
- YouTube and video creation: Building a YouTube channel, creating engaging videos, and earning income through advertising revenue, brand partnerships, and product endorsements.
- Podcasting: Creating and hosting a podcast, monetizing through sponsorships, advertising, or premium content.

Section 5: Cryptocurrencies and Blockchain Technology

- Understanding cryptocurrencies: Exploring the potential of digital currencies like Bitcoin, Ethereum, or Litecoin, and learning about blockchain technology.
- Trading and investing: Participating in cryptocurrency trading or investing in blockchain-based projects to capitalize on the growth of the digital asset market.
- Blockchain-based businesses: Identifying opportunities to develop or invest in businesses utilizing blockchain technology, such as decentralized finance (DeFi), non-fungible tokens (NFTs), or smart contracts.

Section 6: Automation and Scalability

- Embracing automation tools: Leveraging automation tools and software to streamline business processes, save time, and increase productivity.
- Scaling your online ventures: Identifying strategies to scale your online business, such as outsourcing tasks, expanding your reach, or diversifying your product/service offerings.

Conclusion: The digital age offers an unparalleled opportunity to leverage technology for wealth creation. By embracing e-commerce, affiliate marketing, freelancing, content creation, and exploring the world of cryptocurrencies and blockchain technology, you can tap into the vast potential of the digital landscape. Embrace the power of automation and scalability to maximize your efficiency and reach. However, it is crucial to stay informed, adapt to emerging technologies, and continually refine your skills to remain competitive. With an entrepreneurial mindset and a willingness to embrace digital tools and platforms, you can harness the power of technology to unlock new levels of financial success in the digital age.

CHAPTER 5: NURTURING RELATIONSHIPS AND NETWORKING

Building strong relationships and cultivating a robust network is a vital component of achieving financial success. This chapter explores the significance of nurturing relationships, establishing connections, and leveraging your network to create opportunities and accelerate your wealth-building journey.

Section 1: The Power of Relationships

- Recognizing the value of relationships: Understanding that genuine and meaningful connections can provide support, guidance, and access to valuable resources.
- Building trust and credibility: Cultivating trust and credibility by consistently demonstrating integrity, reliability, and a genuine interest in others.
- Fostering a giving mindset: Embracing a mindset of giving and providing value to others without expecting immediate returns.

Section 2: Networking Strategies

- Expanding your network: Actively seeking opportunities to meet new people, whether in-person or online, through industry events, conferences, social media platforms, or professional organizations.
- Effective communication: Developing strong

communication skills, including active listening, empathy, and effective storytelling, to connect with others on a deeper level.

- Leveraging social media: Utilizing platforms like LinkedIn, Twitter, or Facebook to connect with professionals in your industry, share insights, and engage in meaningful conversations.

Section 3: Mentorship and Guidance

- Seeking mentors: Identifying individuals who have achieved success in your desired field and seeking their guidance and mentorship.
- Establishing mentor-mentee relationships: Nurturing relationships with mentors by being receptive to feedback, showing gratitude, and actively implementing their advice.
- Peer-to-peer learning: Engaging with a community of like-minded individuals who are also on a journey toward financial success, providing support, and exchanging knowledge and experiences.

Section 4: Collaboration and Partnerships

- Collaborative projects: Exploring opportunities to collaborate with others in your industry or complementary fields to create mutually beneficial projects or ventures.
- Joint ventures and partnerships: Identifying potential partners or businesses with shared goals and values to leverage collective strengths and resources.
- Networking events and mastermind groups: Participating in networking events or joining mastermind groups to connect with individuals who can contribute to your growth and provide valuable insights.

Section 5: Building a Personal Brand

- Defining your personal brand: Identifying your unique strengths, expertise, and values, and crafting a compelling personal brand that differentiates you from others.

- Online presence: Establishing a strong online presence through a professional website, social media profiles, and thought leadership content to enhance your credibility and visibility.
- Thought leadership and expertise: Sharing your knowledge and expertise through speaking engagements, writing articles, hosting webinars, or appearing as a guest on podcasts to position yourself as an authority in your field.

Section 6: Maintaining and Nurturing Relationships

- Consistent communication: Regularly staying in touch with your network through emails, phone calls, or in-person meetings to maintain connections and foster long-term relationships.
- Adding value: Continuously seeking opportunities to provide value to your network through introductions, sharing resources, or offering support and guidance.
- Reciprocity and gratitude: Expressing gratitude and reciprocating support when others in your network offer assistance or opportunities.

Conclusion: Nurturing relationships and networking are essential elements of your wealth-building journey. By recognizing the power of relationships, expanding your network, seeking mentorship, fostering collaboration, building a personal brand, and maintaining connections, you can create a strong support system and open doors to new opportunities. Remember, genuine relationships are built on trust, respect, and mutual support. Cultivate meaningful connections, add value to others, and embrace the power of collaboration. Through the strength of your relationships, you can amplify your financial success, gain valuable insights, and create a network that propels you towards your goals.

CHAPTER 6: ACHIEVING FINANCIAL FREEDOM AND LONG-TERM WEALTH

The ultimate goal of building wealth is to attain financial freedom and create a secure and abundant future. This chapter focuses on strategies to achieve long-term wealth, cultivate a mindset of abundance, and attain true financial independence.

Section 1: Setting Financial Goals

- Defining your vision of financial freedom: Clarifying your long-term financial goals, aspirations, and the lifestyle you desire.
- SMART goal setting: Setting Specific, Measurable, Achievable, Relevant, and Time-bound goals to create a roadmap for your financial journey.
- Breaking down goals into milestones: Breaking down your long-term goals into smaller, actionable steps to track progress and stay motivated.

Section 2: Building and Preserving Wealth

- Wealth accumulation strategies: Continuously saving and investing a portion of your income to build wealth over time.
- Diversification and asset allocation: Spreading your investments across different asset classes, such as stocks, bonds, real estate, and commodities, to mitigate risk and

maximize returns.

- Tax-efficient investing: Understanding and implementing strategies to optimize your investment returns by minimizing tax liabilities.

Section 3: Creating Passive Income Streams

- Leveraging passive income opportunities: Exploring avenues such as rental properties, dividend-paying stocks, royalties, or income from digital products to generate passive income.
- Developing residual income: Building businesses or investments that generate ongoing income even when you're not actively working.
- Reinvesting for compound growth: Reinvesting the income generated from your passive investments to accelerate wealth accumulation through the power of compounding.

Section 4: Managing Risk and Protecting Wealth

- Insurance and risk management: Evaluating your insurance needs and protecting your assets and income with appropriate coverage, such as life insurance, health insurance, and property insurance.
- Estate planning: Creating a comprehensive estate plan to ensure the smooth transfer of wealth, minimize estate taxes, and protect your legacy for future generations.
- Asset protection strategies: Implementing legal and financial measures to shield your assets from potential risks or lawsuits.

Section 5: Cultivating a Mindset of Abundance and Financial Independence

- Shifting your mindset: Adopting a mindset of abundance, gratitude, and positivity to attract wealth and create a sense of financial independence.
- Financial education and continuous learning: Investing in your financial education by reading books, attending seminars, and staying informed about personal finance

and investment strategies.

- Embracing delayed gratification: Practicing disciplined spending and saving habits, prioritizing long-term financial goals over short-term impulses.

Section 6: Giving Back and Leaving a Legacy

- Philanthropy and charitable giving: Incorporating a giving component into your wealth-building journey by supporting causes and organizations aligned with your values.
- Legacy planning: Considering the impact you want to leave on future generations by establishing charitable foundations, trusts, or endowments to support causes you care about.

Conclusion: Achieving financial freedom and long-term wealth requires discipline, strategic planning, and a mindset of abundance. By setting clear financial goals, building and preserving wealth through diversified investments, creating passive income streams, managing risks, and cultivating a mindset of abundance, you can attain true financial independence. Remember to continually educate yourself, adapt to changing circumstances, and align your actions with your long-term goals. As you embark on this journey, embrace the opportunity to give back and leave a lasting legacy. With dedication, perseverance, and a commitment to financial empowerment, you can create a future of financial abundance, freedom, and fulfillment.